# WOMEN OF TODAY: CONTEMPORARY ISSUES AND CONFLICTS 1980–PRESENT

## KAYE STEARMAN AND PATIENCE COSTER

CHELSEA HOUSE
An Infobase Learning Company

Clifton Park - Halfmoon Public Library
475 Moe Road
Clifton Park, New York 12065

WOMEN OF TODAY: CONTEMPORARY ISSUES AND CONFLICTS 1980–PRESENT

Produced for Chelsea House by Bailey Publishing Associates Ltd, 11a Woodlands, Hove BN3 6TJ, England

Library of Congress Cataloging-in-Publication Data
Stearman, Kaye.
  Women of today : contemporary issues and conflicts, 1980-present / Kaye Stearman and Patience Coster.
    p. cm. — (A cultural history of women in America)
  Includes index.
  ISBN 978-1-60413-936-5
  1. Women—United States—Social conditions—21st century—Juvenile literature. 2. Women—United States—Economic conditions—21st century—Juvenile literature. 3. Feminism—United States--History—21st century—Juvenile literature. 4. Feminism—United States—History—20th century—Juvenile literature. 5. United States—Social conditions—1980—Juvenile literature.  I. Coster, Patience. II. Title. III. Series.
  HQ1421.S736 2011
  305.40973'09045—dc22
                                    2010046014

3378

Project management by Patience Coster
Text design by Jane Hawkins
Picture research by Shelley Noronha
Printed and bound in Malaysia
Bound book date: April 2011

10 9 8 7 6 5 4 3 2 1

This book is printed on acid-free paper.

The publishers would like to thank the following for permission to reproduce their pictures:
The Advertising Archives: 15; Corbis: 5 (NASA – digital version copyright/Science Faction), 8 (Diego Goldberg/Sygma), 9 (Frank Polich/Reuters), 10 (JLP/Jose L. Pelaez), 12 (Logan Mock-Bunting/Aurora Photos), 13 (Viviane Moos), 14 (Reuters), 16 (Evan Hurd/Sygma), 18 (JLP/Jose L. Pelaez), 20 (Megan Q. Daniels/First Light), 21 (Rick Wilking/Reuters), 22 (Martha Stewart Living Television/Anders Krusberg/ Hand Out/ Reuters), 23 (Bettmann), 24 (Dan Lamont/epa), 25 (Roger Ressmeyer), 27 (Bettmann), 28 (Condé Nast Archive), 30 (Pablo Rivera/Golden Pixels LLC), 32 (Wally McNamee), 33 (Alison Wright), 34 (Bettmann), 35 (Buddy Mays), 37 (Jeffrey Markowitz/Sygma), 38 (Lucas Jackson/Reuters), 39 (Michael Reynolds/epa), 41 (Jason Reed/Reuters), 42 (Phil McCarten/Reuters), 43 (Reuters), 48 (Chris Kleponis/Reuters), 49 (Bettmann), 50 (Lucas Jackson/Reuters), 54 (Andrew Gombert/epa), 55 (Victor Lerena/epa), 56 (Frédéric de Lafosse/Sygma), 57 (Roger Ressmeyer), 58 (Leonhard Foeger/Reuters); Rex Features: 7 (Sipa Press), 11 (Startraks), 26 (ABC inc/Everett), 29 (Burger/Phanie), 40 (KPA/Zuma), 46 (20th Century Fox/ Everett), 47 (Sipa Press), 52 (HBO/Everett), 59 (Sipa Press); TopFoto: 44 (HIP), 51, 53; TopFoto/ImageWorks: 6, 17, 19, 31, 36, 45.

# CONTENTS

Five hundred years ago, when European women first set foot on American soil, their position in society was very clear. Wives were the property of their husbands and their activities were restricted to the domestic sphere—that of bearing and raising children and looking after the home. These women would not recognize the world today.

Women in the 21st century have rights and a degree of independence that would amaze their 16th-century counterparts. Women of today might find it hard to imagine the restrictions their ancestors had to endure. Over the centuries, women have struggled to achieve equality, and only relatively recently have they won the right to vote. Now, however, they can pursue the career path of their choice. They have scaled the heights of business, the military, and the media. They have entered professions previously barred to them and become politicians, surgeons, mechanics, lawyers, and astronauts. A woman has yet to become president of the United States, but there is now no barrier to this becoming a reality.

In terms of social development, advances in birth control mean that women can choose to have children or remain childless. If they do decide to have children, they can continue working outside the home or remain as stay-at-home moms. But in spite of the improvements to women's lives, inequalities remain. Men occupy the vast majority of top jobs. Generally, women still earn less than men, and more women than men live on welfare.

Unlike their ancestors, today's women face contradictory pressures: they are expected to be superwomen, holding down jobs while at the same time running homes and looking after children. They still shoulder the responsibility for most of the domestic chores and struggle constantly to maintain a satisfactory work–life balance. In the youth-obsessed 21st century, older women face new issues, such as ageism in the workplace. For a modern woman, the sky is the limit: her problem remains one of having the opportunity, time, and confidence to reach for it.

*Left:* To infinity and beyond: in 2007 NASA's chief astronaut, Peggy Whitson, carries out maintenance work on the International Space Station. She was the first female commander of the station. The clouds and oceans of Earth can be seen beneath her.

"

### CAUGHT IN A TRAP?

*"For all the upbeat 'You go, girl' slogans, women remain caught between feminism and femininity, between self-affirmation and an endless quest for self-improvement, between playing the injured party and claiming independence."*

Laura Kipnis, writing in *The Female Thing: Dirt, Sex, Envy, Vulnerability,* 2006

# CHAPTER I

# THE MODERN ERA

BETWEEN 1980 AND THE PRESENT DAY, REAL AND SIGNIFICANT changes have taken place in the quality of women's lives in the United States. Today many more women occupy positions of power and authority, and new laws have been passed to support women's rights. Women have made great strides in the workplace and in education, science, arts, and culture. To understand the background to these changes, it is important to take a look at the legacy of the women's liberation movement.

## WOMEN'S LIBERATION

By 1977, the women's liberation movement, which had been active during the late 1960s and 1970s, seemed to have run its course. Early hopes that the movement would grow to embrace the interests of a broad cross section of women had not been fulfilled. Instead it had split into numerous small factions scattered around the country, which claimed to support different groups of women (such as women of color

### ♥ WOMEN OF COURAGE AND CONVICTION

#### BELLA ABZUG (1920–98)

Bella Abzug trained as a lawyer and became a passionate campaigner for civil and women's rights. She was elected to Congress as a Democratic representative from New York in 1970 and continued in that role until 1977, when she unsuccessfully ran for the Senate. Later she founded the Women's Environment and Development Organization (WEDO) to support women's participation in international decision making.

*Right:* Bella Abzug at a rally in New York City in 1973. Abzug had a forceful personality and was an intrepid campaigner for women's rights. She said: "I've been described as a tough and noisy woman, a prizefighter, a man hater, you name it. . . . But whatever I am . . . I am a very serious woman."

or other minorities) or championed different issues (such as an end to violence against women).

Many of the ideas put forward by women's liberation (or feminism, as it increasingly came to be called) were no longer controversial. Some were widely accepted, even by women who did not consider themselves feminists. These ideas included a belief that women and girls should have equal opportunities in education and at work, including equal pay for women doing the same job as men. There was also widespread support for laws to protect women from violence and harassment at home, at work, and in the community.

## CONFERENCE IN HOUSTON

On November 17, 1977, around 20,000 participants gathered for the Women's National Conference in Houston, Texas. Their aim was to develop a national plan of action to promote equality between women and men. The conference brought together women from all

> ### A LEAP INTO THE UNKNOWN
>
> *"No society has ever had sexual equality and the Equal Rights Amendment, if it succeeds, will be for that reason a leap into the unknown. But it will not be an immediate, revolutionary leap beyond the restraints of law and custom. The ERA would cause change, but it is also an attempt to deal with the changes that are already taking place."*
>
> Jane O'Reilly, journalist, writing in 1976

## TURNING POINT

### THE DEFEAT OF THE EQUAL RIGHTS AMENDMENT

In 1982, the Equal Rights Amendment (ERA) was declared moot (dead) after failing to reach ratification (agreement) by three-quarters of the U.S. states. For women's rights campaigners, this was a bitter blow since they had spent much of the previous decade lobbying to have it accepted. Adding the ERA to the Constitution would have made sex discrimination unlawful. For some people, this defeat symbolized the following decades, during which the United States grew more conservative in terms of politics and the economy.

*Left:* Women march in support of the Equal Rights Amendment in Washington, D.C., in the summer of 1978.

7

states and political backgrounds, including first lady Rosalyn Carter and former first ladies Betty Ford and Lady Bird Johnson.

## AGAINST DISCRIMINATION

The delegates looked closely at twenty-six areas of women's lives. They urged the government to create and enforce laws on equal opportunity, equal pay, and equal right to credit (such as bank accounts and loans). They said that women should be treated the same as men in the workplace and that there should be more part-time and flexible jobs to suit women's lifestyles. They also argued that there should be no discrimination on grounds of marital status or pregnancy.

These topics were at the heart of many of the changes that would take place in women's lives over the following thirty years. Since 1980, few events have dramatically altered the course of women's history. Most changes have been gradual, affecting families and communities rather than laws and governments; nevertheless, they have been significant both for women and for men.

*Below*: Nancy Reagan, pictured with President Ronald Reagan in 1985. This first lady was best known for her expensive, stylish clothes and celebrity friends, but she was also one of her husband's most trusted advisers.

## FIRST LADIES

Although the United States has never had a woman president, some of the first ladies of this era have been very influential. President Ronald Reagan's wife, Nancy (first lady from 1980–88), was noted for her fashion style. In most respects she seemed to be a traditional wife, but it was later revealed she had a strong influence on President Reagan's policies. Barbara Bush, first lady to President George Bush (1989–92), was seen as maternal, friendly, and approachable. Her daughter-in-law, Laura Bush (wife of President George W. Bush, 2001–2009), spoke out on the rights of women in Afghanistan and Iraq, but only in relation to her husband's policy of prosecuting a war in those countries.

In contrast, Hillary Rodham Clinton was actively involved in political life, especially during President Bill Clinton's first term (1993–96), when she drew up plans for health-care reform. She has gone on to have a successful political career, first as a senator from New York and then as secretary of state under President Barack Obama. Michelle Obama gave up a successful legal career to become first lady and works to encourage girls from all backgrounds to aim high in life.

*Above:* Oprah Winfrey reacts to the crowd during the taping of an episode of the twenty-fourth season of her television show in 2009.

## ROLE MODELS

By the early 21st century, it seemed that few walks of life were off-limits to women. There were prominent female role models in law and politics, including Supreme Court judges Sandra Day O'Connor and Sonia Sotomayor, secretaries of state Madeleine Albright and Condoleezza Rice, and Speaker of the House of Representatives Nancy Pelosi. In the media, it used to be thought that news anchor was too important a job to entrust to a woman. Today, anchorwomen such as Katie Couric and Diane Sawyer front nightly television news broadcasts.

Women have also moved in on another male-dominated area—computer science. In 2007, Frances Allen won the Turing Award, considered the Nobel Prize of computing. Barbara Liskov, head of the Programming Methodology Group at the Massachusetts Institute of Technology (MIT), received the award in 2009. In 2010, in the almost exclusively male world of motor sports, Anna Chatten became the first woman to work in a pit crew for a female driver in the Indianapolis 500.

> ### BREAKTHROUGH BIOGRAPHY
>
> #### OPRAH WINFREY (1954– )
>
> Oprah Winfrey's childhood was marred by loss, abuse, and hardship. Born to an unwed teenage mother, she spent her early years in the care of her grandmother on a Mississippi farm. At age six she went to live with her mother in Milwaukee. While her mother was out at work during the day, the young Oprah was repeatedly molested by male relatives. At age fourteen she was living on the streets and, while still a teenager, gave birth to a baby boy who died in infancy.
>
> Finally, Oprah went to live in Tennessee with her father, Vernon, who gave her the structured environment she needed to thrive. She achieved at school and at age seventeen won a beauty pageant. She was subsequently offered a job in local radio. She made the move from radio to television and was given her own talk show in 1984. In addition to being open and honest about her own life, Oprah dealt with difficult and highly personal subjects, such as marriage and family breakdown, gay rights, and HIV/AIDS. Her show appealed especially to black and other minority women, who could identify with Oprah's struggles, but it also crossed racial, ethnic, and gender lines. For a quarter of a century, *The Oprah Winfrey Show* has remained one of the top-ranking television programs in the United States.

# CHAPTER 2

# FAMILY AND SOCIETY

A WOMAN'S ROLE IN THE FAMILY HAS NOT altered much in the past thirty years. During the day, most adults are out at work or in the home, while children are at school. Women still do most of the domestic chores, though some men do more than they used to around the home. Today many more women go out to work. They achieve this through a more equal sharing of responsibilities with their partners or by hiring in help with the child care and housework.

*Below*: In a society where both parents are often out at work, an increasing number of grandparents are called on to act as part-time caregivers for their grandchildren.

## LIFE EXPECTANCY

In 2008, there were 152,800,000 women and girls in the United States—50.7 percent of the population. There were more women than ever before, not only as a result of the rising population but also because of increased life expectancy. In 1900, women could expect to live only to fifty. By 1950, women's life expectancy had risen to seventy-one. By 2000, it had risen to seventy-nine and was forecast to rise further.

### C. NOEL BAIREY MERZ (1956– )

Dr. C. Noel Bairey Merz deals with one of the most urgent health problems affecting American women—heart disease. As chair of the National Heart, Lung and Blood Institute since 1997, she has investigated the diagnoses and treatment of women's heart disease. Studies show that women often have different symptoms of heart disease than men and that these are less likely to be recognized by doctors. At the Cedars-Sinai Medical Center in Los Angeles, Dr. Merz works to ensure that doctors are aware of early symptoms of heart disease and give women prompt and appropriate treatment.

*Above:* Dr. C. Noel Bairey Merz (left), pictured with businessman Michael Gould and singer and actress Barbra Streisand at a fundraising event for the Cedars-Sinai Medical Center in 2010.

In 1900, one of the biggest dangers women faced was pregnancy and childbirth. By 2000, these health hazards had been greatly reduced.

## MARRIAGE, COHABITATION, AND DIVORCE

In the 20th century, the nuclear family—husband and wife and two or three children—was the norm. Women married young and had children soon after. Husbands went out to work, and wives stayed home to raise the children, perhaps combining their chores with a part-time or volunteer job.

By 2010, this pattern had changed substantially. On the whole, women were marrying later. In 1900, the average marrying age was twenty; by 2005, it was twenty-six. One reason women are waiting longer to marry is that new opportunities have opened up in education and careers.

### TURNING POINT

### GREATER IN NUMBER

In May 1981, the U.S. Census reported that, as of April 1980, there were six million more women than men in the United States. The main reason for this was that women, on average, lived several years longer than men. In the over sixty-five age group, there were three women for every two men.

*Above*: Welcoming a new family member: many women enjoy being full-time moms. However, mothers often feel pressured to return to paid work soon after giving birth, particularly in times of economic recession.

TURNING POINT

## MATERNAL MORTALITY RATES RISE AGAIN

While the mortality (death) rates for babies have fallen steadily, during the 21st century, mortality rates have risen for mothers. Between 1982 and 1996, there were seven or eight deaths for every 100,000 women giving birth. By 2006, the number of deaths had climbed to thirteen per 100,000 births, with black and other minority women three times more likely to die than white women. Although standards of medical care are high, it is hard for the poorest women to get good treatment because it is costly.

Women want to establish a career before settling down to have a family. An increasing number are choosing to remain single and childless.

Another reason is that many couples decide to live together—or cohabit—outside marriage. Earlier generations regarded this type of living arrangement as socially unacceptable, but by 1980, attitudes had begun to change. The number of couples cohabiting rose threefold between 1960 and 1983; by 2007, it had increased tenfold. In a relatively short time, cohabitation had become socially acceptable and was often seen as part of a natural progression, possibly leading to marriage and children. Also, lesbians, who in the past might have hidden their sexuality, became more open in their lifestyles, perhaps forming a family unit with their partners and children.

Compared to many Western societies, the United States has high divorce rates. By the end of the 20th century, divorce and remarriage had begun to lose much of their social stigma. Rather than being seen as something shameful, divorce became a way of rectifying a mistake and moving on. Most divorced people, women and men, do remarry—some several times.

## SHARING DOMESTIC CHORES

When it comes to housework, inequality is still the rule, with women shouldering the greater burden. Nevertheless, there have been significant changes. In 1965, a survey found that men did around four hours of domestic chores each week, plus two hours of child care. A similar survey in 2003 found that men did around nine hours of housework each week and seven hours of child care.

However, women still did much more. In 1965, they spent an average of thirty-two hours a week on housework and fourteen hours on child care. Over the next forty years, while the amount of time spent on child care remained more or less the same, the time women spent on housework was reduced dramatically to just over eighteen hours a week. This was partly because women working outside the home had less time for chores. A minority of wealthier employed a house cleaner—usually a woman getting low wages.

## DOMESTIC VIOLENCE

Violence against women—wives, partners, mothers, and daughters—by family members continues to be a common problem. Once it was hidden or secretly accepted, but today it is widely condemned and punishable by law. Women fleeing domestic violence are offered temporary accommodation and support in shelters. In 1977, there were just thirty shelters; in 2008, there were over 2,000.

## HOMELESSNESS

Homelessness can have a devastating effect on women and children. According to the National Coalition for the Homeless, there has been a dramatic increase in homelessness over the last twenty-five years, with a sharp rise from 2008, when millions of families lost their

> ## FREE TO CHOOSE
>
> *"Today there are more options. Women who are financially independent may choose to bear or adopt children with or without a husband and, in most communities, without stigma. Married or not, they may choose a child-free life. These choices are made possible by the widespread availability of contraception. My generation was the first to have access to the pill and other effective forms of birth control."*
>
> In 1997, Sarah B. Kreps, a writer and editor, compared the experience of her generation to that of her mother.

*Below*: Life is tough when you have no permanent place to live. A mother and her son find temporary accommodation at the Lydia E. Hoffman Family Residence in the Bronx, New York, a shelter for homeless families.

homes through foreclosures. The fastest-growing sector of the homeless population is families with children, and two-thirds of these are female-headed families. In addition to poverty and unemployment, many of these women have suffered domestic violence at the hands of their partners.

## MINORITY GROUPS

Not all women have an equal chance of reaching a happy and healthy old age. African-American, Hispanic, and other minority women tend to die younger than white women. For example, in 2003 white women could expect to live to over age eighty and black women to seventy-six. The group with the lowest life expectancy was Native American women.

> ### BREAKTHROUGH BIOGRAPHY
>
> ### MARTINA NAVRATILOVA (1956– )
>
> Martina Navratilova has been described as the greatest-ever female tennis player, excelling at both singles and doubles. During her long professional career, she has won fifty-nine Grand Slam titles—eighteen singles, thirty-one women's doubles, and ten mixed doubles. But she is much more than a great sports star. Born in Czechoslovakia, at the age of eighteen she asked for political asylum in the United States to escape the rigid restrictions of her homeland, and later gained U.S. citizenship. She has been open about her lesbian relationships, despite the risk of possible damage to her career. She has supported many causes, including animal welfare, civil rights, and gay and lesbian rights.
>
> *Right:* Tennis champion Martina Navratilova, pictured at the moment when she won her eighth Wimbledon singles title in 1987.

The reasons are complex but relate to poverty, poor diet and living conditions, and lack of access to good health care and health insurance.

## PRESSURES OF MODERN LIFE

Life is still a challenge even for women from wealthier socio-economic groups. The modern woman not only has to combine work and family duties but is also expected to look good. The physical ideal is defined largely by advertising and the media, in campaigns, "self-help" books, and articles in magazines and on the Internet. Often written by women, these articles give the impression of offering constructive support to the reader. However, they are generally counsels of perfection that exploit a woman's unhappiness and discomfort with her own body image. "You can do better than this!" they cry, exhorting the reader to lose weight by following the latest diet fad, remain young by buying the most expensive anti-aging cream, and keep healthy by taking up the newest fitness regime.

## BACKLASH

By the 1990s, many people felt the time had come to make a case against the women's liberation movement of the 1970s. They saw feminism as dreary and hectoring. A symptom of the backlash against feminism was the growth of a market in lad magazines. Aimed at young men who found feminized "new men" dull and weak, publications such as *Maxim*, *Stuff*, and *FHM* adopted a jokey, macho, swaggering tone. Their main selling point was the inclusion of images of scantily-clad women—conforming to a strict notion of female beauty—who were presented as objects to be enjoyed by male readers. The magazines sold extremely well, which prompted other media to follow their lead. Similar photographs began to be seen in women's and

---

*Right:* Women's physical insecurities have long been exploited to sell products. But this ad from the 1990s targets the male as much as the female consumer.

> "

## TOO MUCH PRESSURE

*"I feel like I'm pretending at work that I don't have a family and pretending at home that I don't have a job."*

Mureille Soria, interviewed in 1996 for a book called *Work Matters*, by Sara Ann Friedman. Many of those interviewed struggled to balance paid work with domestic duties.

VICTORIA'S SECRET

*Right:* Heavily made-up young girls take part in a beauty pageant in the 1990s. Many people argue that such competitions teach girls from an early age that their self-worth is measured by how pretty they are.

## EATING DISORDERS

"Up to one-tenth of all young American women, up to one-fifth of women students . . . are locked into one-woman hunger camps. . . . Anorexia and bulimia are female maladies. . . . 90 to 95 percent of anorexics and bulimics are women. America, which has the greatest number of women who have made it into the male sphere, also leads the world with female anorexia."

In 1990, Naomi Wolf wrote *The Beauty Myth*, which investigated the impact of the fashion and beauty industries. She argued that women's lives and personalities were damaged by the pressure they felt to be ever youthful and beautiful. Eating disorders, she said, were a consequence of this pressure to be perfect.

girls' magazines and on television. People who expressed distaste at these images were regarded as out of touch and humorless.

## GIRLS AND SELF-ESTEEM

In the 21st century, the preoccupation with image and appearance begins early on. This is partly because girls mature at a younger age, but it also reflects the way marketing and advertising target preteens to sell clothes, makeup, and "lifestyle" products. Many people regard this as sexualizing girls, shortening their childhood and making them look and act older than their real age. This is problematic, because mentally and emotionally they are still children. The sexualization of young girls can push them into early sexual relationships and may make them prey to the advances of older men.

As girls enter their teenage years they worry increasingly about whether they are sufficiently thin, pretty, "cool," and fashionable. This anxiety about appearance may be a reason for the increase in the number of girls suffering from eating disorders such as anorexia and bulimia. Eating disorders are now so common in the United States that two students out of every hundred are likely to suffer from one.

## DROPOUT RATES

Over the past thirty years, high school dropout rates have decreased considerably. However, girls from lower-income families and some minority groups drop out more frequently, although not as often as boys from the same groups. This is especially true for African-American, Hispanic, and Native American girls, who are also more likely to live in neighborhoods where schools are overcrowded or lower quality.

## TEENAGE PREGNANCY

Girls who drop out of high school give a variety of reasons for doing so. A major reason for dropping out of education on a long-term basis is pregnancy and caring for a baby. Becoming a mother has a huge impact on a girl's education. Although they are entitled to remain in school, many teen mothers drop out, finding it impossible to juggle the demands of education with caring for a baby. If they stay, they may find themselves being excluded or bullied rather than included and supported. Sometimes they may be forced to attend a special "pregnancy school," which separates them from mainstream education.

*Below:* A teenage mother tends to her young baby. The United States has the highest teen pregnancy rate in the industrialized world.

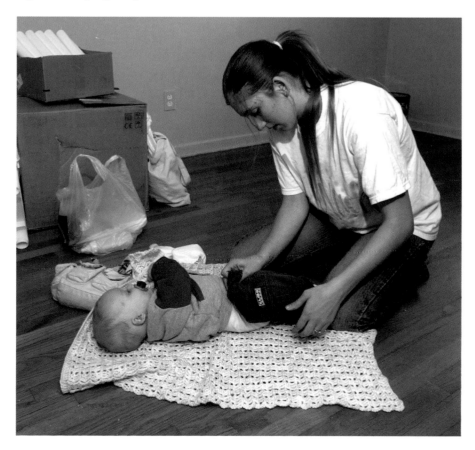

### TURNING POINT

### MS. GAINS ACCEPTANCE

In the 1970s, many women chose to use the title Ms., rather than Miss or Mrs., to avoid revealing whether they were single or married (in the same way men used Mr.). In the 1980s, this became more widely accepted. In 1986, the *New York Times* finally accepted Ms. as a title for use. Many other newspapers had stopped using titles altogether and instead referred to people by their names alone.

### TURNING POINT

### COSMETIC SURGERY

During the 1990s, many American women began to see cosmetic surgery as a safe and desirable way to change their appearance. Previously, cosmetic surgery had been mainly limited to older, wealthier women and movie stars. But falling prices, the development of procedures such as Botox (injections into the skin), and a new openness about the use of cosmetic surgery mean that it has rapidly become more acceptable. In 1997, two million cosmetic procedures were done; in 2007, the number had risen to over eleven million.

# CHAPTER 3

# EDUCATION AND ACHIEVEMENT

I N TERMS OF EDUCATION, YOUNG WOMEN SEEM TO BE BETTER OFF today than ever before. Most girls are from secure and loving families and have a good standard of living. They attend school, where many do well and achieve high grades. Some women, such as sports stars, offer a positive role model for girls. Of course, there remain obstacles and pressures to overcome but, compared with previous generations, girls now seem to experience little discrimination in their daily lives.

*Below:* Students in a school biology class. Despite an increase in the number of young women studying science at college, most of them favor biology and related sciences. Fewer girls than boys go on to study subjects such as physics and engineering.

## GIRLS AT SCHOOL

For generations, most girls have been educated alongside boys in local public schools. At elementary school level, it is well-documented that girls learn to read and write faster than boys and are more sociable and cooperative. These results carry over into high school. In 1980, almost 35 percent of girls graduated from high school; the figure rose to 75

*Above:* High achievers: young women attend their graduation ceremony at Fowler High School in Syracuse, New York, in 2008.

percent by 1990 and was over 80 percent by 2000, slightly higher than the figure for boys.

## COLLEGE AND HIGHER EDUCATION

Fifty years ago, most parents believed a college education was more important for boys than for girls. This is no longer the case; today many girls go on to higher education. Since the 1950s, this sector has steadily expanded, and many more high-school graduates now enroll in college for both two- and four-year degree programs.

In 1960, 750,000 high-school students enrolled in college. In 1980, this number had doubled to 1.5 million. Numbers then grew more slowly, reaching 1.8 million in 2005. Many of these new places went to young women. In 1960, 54 percent of young men enrolled in college compared with 38 percent of young women. In 1980, women had overtaken men, with just 46.7 percent of men enrolling compared with 51.8 percent of women. In the 21st century, the numbers of women have risen in nearly all areas of education, across most types of degrees

### TURNING POINT

## THE IMPACT OF THE INTERNET

During the 1990s, the system of communication known as the Internet entered the lives of ordinary people. At school and socially, girls became devoted users of the Internet. In 2000, researchers said that girls between the ages of twelve and seventeen were the fastest-growing group of Internet users. While boys used the Internet mainly for downloading games and music, girls were more likely to use it for social activities such as e-mails, instant messaging, online teen magazines, and social-networking web sites.

*Above*: Women have made inroads into professions traditionally associated with men. This civil engineer stands in front of a water filtration system in Chapel Hill, North Carolina.

and across different racial and ethnic groups. Women are steadily becoming more educationally successful than men.

## REASONS TO STUDY

One reason that girls want to secure a good education is because college degrees lead to better-paid jobs. Today more jobs require degrees and diplomas, especially in the "caring professions" such as teaching, nursing, and social work, where women dominate.

Young women also seek qualifications in less traditionally female areas, such as the law, finance, and business. The number of women studying traditionally "male" subjects, such as science and engineering, has also risen. In 2001, about 40 percent of students gaining undergraduate degrees in these areas were women. However, most female science students majored in biology and psychology rather than computer science and engineering.

Girls go to college for other reasons, too. It offers opportunities for them to see and explore the wider world and socialize with different groups of people. Unlike young women in previous generations, girls today are under less pressure to marry and settle down early in life. They have more positive role models of women who have combined high academic achievement with work and family.

## SINGLE-SEX SCHOOLING

There has been much debate about the advantages and disadvantages of single-sex education. In 1972, it was declared that schools receiving federal funding could not discriminate on the basis of sex. This was seen as a victory for the women's rights movement. All-male education used to be regarded by some feminists as a means by which men gained better education and employment and greater power. However, there is now a debate about whether single-sex education is in fact better for girls. In May 2002, the federal government, under the No Child Left Behind Act, relaxed its guidelines concerning the separation of sexes. Single-sex classrooms are now allowed.

## SEX EDUCATION

Although sex and relationship education is more readily available now than it was in the past, ignorance about sex and contraception is still

*Left*: A father presents his daughter with her great-grandmother's ring at the annual Father–Daughter Purity Ball in Colorado Springs. At the ball, fathers recite and sign a covenant making them responsible for their daughters' purity. Despite such rituals, the United States has one of the highest teenage pregnancy rates in the developed world.

widespread. Teens acquire information from friends and the Internet, and it can often be wrong or misleading. As a result, teenage girls are at risk of pregnancy or from catching sexually transmitted diseases.

An influential development in the United States, the "virginity movement" advises against sex before marriage and warns against teaching children about any form of birth control other than abstinence (refraining from sex completely.) The danger of this is that schoolchildren are denied access to contraceptive advice, which results in an increase in the number of unwanted pregnancies. By 2000, only 55 percent of teachers in U.S. high schools were teaching pupils how to use a condom. The abstinence approach does not appear to work in practice. Teen pregnancy rates are much higher in the United States than in other rich nations. For example, American teens are twice as likely to become pregnant as those in the United Kingdom and eight times more likely than Dutch teenagers.

## ACHIEVEMENTS

Greater equality in education has produced a wealth of talented, high-achieving women. Greater equality in employment means that women now work in professions that used to be the sole preserve of men. Some

"

### GIRLS GO ONLINE

*"Excuse me, but she had a valid question and you had no right to insult her like that. This is a message board for all girls. Girls have it hard enough already, don't they? Let's not make it worse by picking on each other."*

egodream, writing in the Pow(d) er Room on gURL.com, 1995. The Internet has made it possible for girls to communicate with one another across distance and social barriers, using a name of their choice. Chat rooms are a popular way to ask and answer questions and contribute views. Here, egodream urges contributors to show respect for other girls.

TURNING POINT

## UNITED STATES V. VIRGINIA

In 1996, a ruling by the Supreme Court forced two public military schools—Virginia Military Institute (VMI) and The Citadel—to admit women. The decision struck down any law that denied women equal opportunity to aspire, achieve, participate in, and contribute to society. VMI was the last all-male public school in the United States.

*BREAKTHROUGH BIOGRAPHY*

## MARTHA STEWART (1941– )

For millions of American women, Martha Stewart was the "perfect homemaker, cook, and decorator," a role promoted through the magazine she owned and via her television programs and web site and sales of her brand-name goods. Her television show, which was launched in 1993, was one of the first "makeover shows," although its aim was not a quick fix but a permanent state of perfection. Even a trial on fraud-related charges and a prison sentence in 2004 failed to stop her success. While she may have inspired many women, others see her as promoting an idealized and unrealistic view of domestic life.

of these women, such as architect Joan Goody, were lucky enough to have supportive parents who encouraged their daughters to aim for the top. "There was no suggestion," said Goody, "that I should be playing with dollhouses instead of designing houses." Architect and sculptor Maya Lin, who designed the famous black granite Vietnam Veterans Memorial, also came from an artistic, academic background.

However supportive the background, women still need to possess determination and courage to succeed. Jeana Yeager acquired her pilot's license in 1978. In 1986, she co-piloted a non-stop, non-refueled flight around the world in a specially designed aircraft. She also drafted the engineering drawings and ran the business side of the project, keeping it financially viable.

## WOMEN IN INDUSTRY

The number of women heading business corporations has increased dramatically in the last thirty years. Women now lead publishing empires, financial institutions, cosmetics companies, television stations,

*Below*: Martha Stewart (right) fronted one of the first "makeover shows" on U.S. television. Here she appears with actress Marcia Cross demonstrating the correct way to fold a T-shirt on the premiere episode of her "how-to" series in 2005.

pharmaceuticals groups, restaurant chains, and computer firms. *Forbes* business magazine listed Sheila Bair, the chairman of the Federal Deposit Insurance Corporation, as the second most powerful woman in the world in 2009 (after German chancellor Angela Merkel). Third was Indra Nooyi, chief executive of the giant food corporation PepsiCo.

## ACTIVISM

Women have also made their mark in the field of activism. Elouise Cobell, a banker, is a Native American leader who has achieved some success in challenging the United States' mismanagement of trust funds belonging to more than 500,000 Native Americans. Hispanic environmental engineer Margarita Colmenares won recognition in the 1980s and 1990s working on cleanup projects for the oil company Chevron. Winona LaDuke is an activist on environmental racism and green issues. Environmental racism refers to the disproportionate share of environmental devastation carried out in communities of color. LaDuke campaigns against the targeting of Native American lands for uranium mining, strip mining, mercury contamination, toxic waste dumping, and nuclear bomb testing. She says: "To not struggle is to lose your will."

## SCIENCE AND EDUCATION

Women have triumphed in science and education. In 1981, scientist Flossie Wong-Staal co-discovered HIV, the virus that causes AIDS. Her

### ♥ *WOMEN OF COURAGE AND CONVICTION*

#### JOAN BENOIT
#### (1957– )

In 1984, Joan Benoit made history as the winner of the first Women's Olympic Marathon in Los Angeles. For decades, the Olympic Committee had excluded women's sporting events, including long-distance running, but with women successfully taking part in competitive road races in Europe and America, they could do so no longer. Benoit had won the Boston Marathon in 1979 and 1983, the latter in a world record time of 2 hours, 22 minutes, and 43 seconds and by 1984 was established as one of the world's leading marathon runners. She won her Olympic title 430 meters ahead of the then world champion, Greta Waitz of Norway. She later withdrew from competitive running because of injuries but still remains involved in women's marathon events.

*Left*: At Edwards Air Force base in California, co-pilots Jeana Yeager (left) and Dick Rutan wave to a cheering crowd after completing their non-stop flight around the world in 1986.

*Above*: Biologist Linda B. Buck was the joint recipient of the 2004 Nobel Prize in Physiology or Medicine for her work on the sense of smell. She attributes her success to her upbringing: "I was fortunate to have wonderfully supportive parents who ... taught me to think independently and to be critical of my own ideas."

## TURNING POINT

### WOMEN'S STUDIES

The first women's studies course started in 1970 at San Diego College as a response to the demands of the women's liberation movement for courses about women's history and life experiences. Many more colleges followed suit, and women's studies has since become an academic discipline in its own right. By 2010, there were over four hundred women's studies courses being taught at U.S. colleges and universities.

## TURNING POINT

### MISSISSIPPI UNIVERSITY FOR WOMEN V. HOGAN

In 1979, Joe Hogan, a registered nurse, applied to study at the Mississippi University for Women. The single-sex college refused to admit him, and Hogan filed an action in the district court, arguing that the single-sex admissions policy violated his 14th Amendment right to equal protection. In 1982, the court found in Hogan's favor, and the university was required to change its admissions policy to admit men. *Mississippi University for Women v. Hogan* proved to be an early landmark case in the history of gender equality.

subsequent work with HIV/AIDS involved the search for a cure for AIDS and a vaccine for HIV. Alexa Canady was the first woman and first African American to become a neurosurgeon. She is the director of neurosurgery at the Children's Hospital in Detroit and a clinical associate professor at Wayne State University. Linda Buck worked on mapping the genes and nerve connections behind the sense of smell. She and her former laboratory supervisor at Columbia University, Richard Axel, shared the Nobel Prize in Physiology or Medicine in 2004 for this research. Suzanne Ildstad, a surgeon turned researcher and specialist in organ transplants, has made discoveries that may lead to breakthroughs in organ transplantation and new treatments for AIDS, diabetes, and other conditions.

In the field of publishing, Jan Davidson has developed software for educational titles in math, science, history, reading, and writing and games for children from preschool through 12th grade. Her products have won awards for excellence from educational organizations. In 1999, she and her husband founded the Davidson Institute for Talent Development, a nonprofit organization, to recognize, nurture, and support gifted young people.

## ASTRONOMERS

Records of women's involvement in astronomy date back to Hypatia of Egypt, who invented the astrolabe around 400 B.C. In the mid-2000s, Margaret Geller carried out research into mapping the distant universe to determine the evolution of its structure and attempting to understand the distribution of "dark matter." Sandra Faber helped develop several important theories that explain the formation and movement of galaxies. She also played a significant role in improving the technology by which astronomers study outer space. Faber was a member of the team that designed the Hubble Space Telescope, and she helped diagnose and solve a problem with the Hubble's mirror after the telescope had been deployed in space.

*Below*: Margaret Geller stands in front of a background computer-generated photograph of galactic clusters. In 1993, Geller determined the positions of these galaxies relative to our own Milky Way.

# CHAPTER 4

# WORK

T HE IMAGE OF FAMILY LIFE THAT EMERGED AFTER WORLD WAR II continues to have a strong impact on Americans. It was of a nuclear family, with a father working full time and a mother as a homemaker and caregiver. However, attitudes changed from the 1970s on, with many women taking on full-time paid jobs and challenging careers.

## TURNING POINT

## TAKE OUR DAUGHTERS TO WORK DAY

Some women felt that the greatest barrier to female equality in the workplace was the widespread belief that there were "men's jobs" and "women's jobs." Take Our Daughters to Work Day was launched in 1992 by the Ms. Foundation for Women as an attempt to introduce girls to opportunities in the workplace and to help overcome gender stereotypes about jobs. Take Our Daughters to Work Day is now a regular event on the American calendar. Every April, employers, schools, and community groups participate to make it a success.

*Above:* In 2005, the TV series *Desperate Housewives* addressed the issue of the modern working mom, struggling to balance family and business commitments.

## EARNING A LIVING

Until the 1970s a woman might work before marriage, maybe even for a short time afterward, but as soon as children arrived, she was usually expected to devote herself entirely to her family. Of course, this was

***WOMEN OF COURAGE AND CONVICTION***

### SALLY RIDE
### (1951– )

Sally Ride became the first American woman astronaut as a crew member on the space shuttle *Challenger* in 1983. She joined NASA in 1978 after obtaining a PhD in physics at Stanford University and supported two earlier space shuttle flights as a member of the ground-control crew. She took a second space flight in 1984. She later became a professor of physics at the University of California.

---

*Left*: Sally Ride communicates with ground control from the flight deck of the space shuttle *Challenger* in orbit around the earth in 1983.

never the whole story. Many women continued to work after getting married and having children. They included professional women, such as doctors and lawyers; those in family businesses; poorer women whose families needed their incomes to make ends meet; and single, widowed, or divorced women who relied on their earnings.

The situation began to change from the 1970s on. While paid work used to be a stopgap between education and marriage, it has now evolved into a long-term commitment, a vital source of income, and, perhaps the biggest change of all, an essential part of a woman's personality and identity. By the 21st century, women had begun to identify themselves by their work and career rather than by their status as wives and mothers.

## A CHANGING ECONOMY

One reason for this change in women's lives was that the American economy had moved from heavy manufacturing industries, which employed mainly men, to a range of service industries. Between 1960 and 2000, the number of people employed in manufacturing fell dramatically. At the same time, there was a huge increase in the number

## BREAKTHROUGH BIOGRAPHY

**DONNA KARAN (1948– )**

Donna Karan is a leading American fashion designer. She showed her first women's clothing collection under her own name in 1985 and went on to build a fashion empire. In 1992, she launched DKNY, a range of affordable clothing aimed at younger women. She plans to makes clothes simple and elegant, while being flexible and easy to care for, to match the lifestyle of the modern working woman.

*Right*: Fashion designer Donna Karan pictured in 1991. Karan started selling clothes on Long Island, New York, at age fourteen.

of jobs providing services. These included jobs in retail, finance, catering, tourism, education, health, and other "caring professions," such as social work.

Women filled many of these so-called pink-collar jobs in the service industries. Between 1960 and 2000, over ten million new jobs for women were created in health and education alone. By the end of the 20th century, women were most likely to be found working in the retail trade, in personal services, and as secretaries, cashiers, nurses, elementary school teachers, bookkeepers, accountants, receptionists, and cooks. In many ways, these were still traditional women-oriented jobs, with the emphasis on "people skills" and customer service. A lot of these jobs were part-time – a factor that worked both to women's advantage (more flexibility, therefore easier to work around family life) and to their disadvantage (lower pay and fewer rights).

## CHANGES IN WOMEN'S LIVES

From the mid-1980s, as women were marrying and having children later, they had more time to progress in their jobs. Rather than having to rely on their husband's paycheck, they earned and contributed to the family and household. If their relationship broke down, they could continue to work and earn.

Importantly, women continued to work because their family needed the income. Although some Americans experienced rising living standards from 1980 on, they also had higher aspirations. Families wanted bigger homes, new furniture, and the latest gadgets; they entertained and traveled more. They were more likely to buy than rent their home, even if they had to pay high mortgage rates. Many wanted to see their children go to college and so they saved for college tuition, while health insurance and medical bills were major expenses for most families.

*Above:* A mother takes her eight-month-old infant to a professional caregiver who will look after the child during the mother's working day.

## TWO-INCOME FAMILIES

This meant there was greater pressure on women to work and contribute to the family income. Increasingly, the two-income family became the norm rather than the exception. In 1900, only 6 percent of married women were in paid employment outside the home. In 1992, this had risen to over half, and by 2003, over 60 percent of married women were either doing full- or part-time work.

## WORKING MOTHERS

Women with young children still face huge problems at work. Maternity leave is brief—by law women are entitled to only six weeks of unpaid leave. Good-quality day care is difficult to find and often expensive. Yet women know that if they stop working for any length of time, they are likely to fall behind in career opportunities and earnings.

Increasingly, young women expect to work almost all of their adult lives. In 1980, 50 percent of women over the age of sixteen were in the labor force, compared with 77 percent of men. By 2010, the figures had reached 60 percent for women, while the male rate had fallen to 72 percent.

**TURNING POINT**

## SEXUAL HARASSMENT

From the 1980s on, sexual harassment at home, at work, and in education became a major public issue. It was debated on talk shows and in women's magazines, featured in movies and television dramas, and became the subject of lawsuits. Most importantly, laws were enacted against sexual harassment. In 2000, 15,836 cases of sexual harassment were filed with the Equal Opportunity Commission.

## WOMEN OF COURAGE AND CONVICTION

### BETTY DUKES (1950– )

When Betty Dukes began working at Wal-Mart in Pittsburg, California, in 1994, she hoped the job would lead to promotion and higher wages. However, after nine years her pay had risen by only 48 cents an hour and she had repeatedly been denied promotion. In 2001, with support from the Impact Foundation, an anti-discrimination organization, she began a legal action for equal pay and opportunity. The case has continued since then and is popularly referred to as "Betty Against Goliath." Its outcome could affect the lives of 1.5 million female Wal-Mart workers worldwide.

### "

### PAY DISCRIMINATION

*"In my view, the Court does not comprehend, or is indifferent to, the invidious [unfair] way which women can be victims of pay discrimination."*

Supreme Court Justice Ruth Bader Ginsburg speaking from the bench in 2007. In that year, the Supreme Court was asked to rule on a case of pay discrimination brought by a woman named Lilly Ledbetter against the Goodyear Tire and Rubber Company. For many years, Ledbetter had been paid less than men doing the same job. Although she lost the case, it led to a new law, the Lilly Ledbetter Fair Pay Act, which became the first bill to be signed into law by President Obama in 2009.

## THE EARNINGS GAP

During the 1980s, although women were increasingly working at the same jobs and for the same hours as men, they did not earn the same amount of money. In 1983, a woman working full time earned about 60 percent of what a man would earn for doing the same job. Over the years, the difference has decreased, but it is still unequal. By 2000, women were earning three-quarters of what men earned.

In some marriages, however, women were reversing traditional roles and earning more than their husbands. In the 1950s, most wives did not work, but today it is the norm. In 1970, just 4 percent of women earned more than their husbands. A 2007 survey found that more than one in five women earned more than their husbands. The main reason was that women's rising levels of education were resulting in better jobs and bigger paychecks.

*Below:* An increasing number of women today are pursuing a career in medicine, becoming dentists, doctors, and medical researchers.

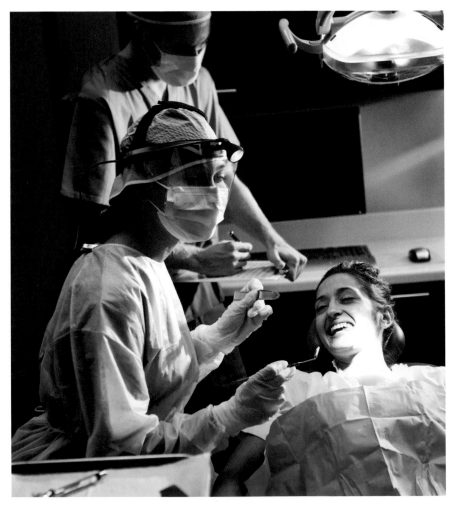

## WOMEN AND MEDICINE

In some professions, women have increased their representation. One example is medicine, often seen as a traditionally male-dominated profession. In 1980, only 25 percent of medical doctors were women, but since then, an greater number of young women have entered the profession. In 1992, 36 percent of medical students were female; in 2006, this number had risen to 49 percent. It is interesting to see medicine becoming an increasingly female profession.

Despite these developments, inequality remains: men still dominate the most prestigious areas of medicine, such as surgery or technical research, where the competition is tough and the hours long. Women doctors, especially those with children, are more likely to specialize in areas such as family medicine, pediatrics (child health), and psychiatry, where the hours are shorter and more regular.

## OTHER PROFESSIONS

There are an increasing number of women in male-dominated professions such as law and finance. But they are still a small minority in other professions, especially those linked to science and engineering. For example, in 2000, the proportion of women airline pilots was just 3.9 percent, and women made up only 12 percent of physicists and astronomers. Women often find themselves facing an unseen barrier—the so-called glass ceiling—that stops them from advancing further.

Women who choose to enter highly skilled jobs, for example in construction or technical roles, or in science and engineering, have found themselves facing social and other barriers. Some old-fashioned employers cannot accept that women can work on equal terms with men. There have been instances of employers refusing to provide facilities for them, such as restrooms or changing rooms. Young women especially have been harassed by male workers or portrayed as unfeminine or unnatural. However, the situation is gradually improving.

*Right:* A changing world: the number of women-owned construction firms grew 20 percent between 1997 and 2002. Today almost 900,000 women work in the U.S. construction industry.

## WOMEN OF COURAGE AND CONVICTION

### KATHERINE GRAHAM (1917–2001)

Katherine Graham was a businesswoman and publisher of the *Washington Post*, which had been previously managed by her father and husband. She took control of the paper in 1963, occupying the position of chairman from 1973 to 1991. She used her influence to support women's advancement and expose corruption in government. She authorized the *Washington Post* to investigate the Watergate scandal of the 1970s, which eventually resulted in the resignation of President Richard Nixon in 1974.

*Below:* Newspaper executive Katherine Graham in her office in Washington, D.C., in 1986.

## WOMEN AT THE TOP

Since 1980, more women have worked in managerial jobs, in charge of people and resources. Many work for small companies or in specialist areas, such as human resources or customer services. Some women are climbing the corporate ladder, and a small number are making it to the top. In 1980, there were no female leaders as president, chairman, or chief executive officer (CEO) of any of the Fortune 500 companies (the 500 largest companies in the United States). In 1985, there was only one woman who made the list—Katherine Graham, CEO of the *Washington Post*. By 1990, the number had risen to five. Almost twenty years later, in 2009, women made up just 15.2 percent of Fortune 500 board directors, with only 3.2 percent of those positions being held by women of color.

## THE "MOMMY TRACK"

Having a high-level job can be very stressful. It is especially hard for those women leaders who try to combine long hours at work with family life. Some decide not to marry or have children, while divorce rates for top-earning women can be high. In the 1990s, a new concept was developed—the so-called "mommy track." The thinking behind this was that companies should not expect businesswomen to combine careers with motherhood and that women should be offered a "mommy track"—jobs that fit in with their family responsibilities but had little opportunity for advancement. Critics say this is discrimination—after all, many men also have family responsibilities but are not offered a "daddy track." Some observers have commented that it is not so much a glass ceiling that prevents women progressing but a labyrinth of twists, turns, and dead ends that stands in the way of more flexible working.

## POORER WOMEN

Those women who get by on severely limited incomes, with little outside support, face even greater stress. In the 1960s, under President Lyndon Johnson, efforts were made to aid poorer families through benefits, education, and housing programs. However, after 1980, many women experienced rising poverty when President Reagan cut government programs for poorer families.

In the 1990s, "workfare" programs introduced under President Clinton ruled that women on welfare should work for their benefits. Supporters said this gave poor women new opportunities to gain training and work experience. But critics argued that the programs forced women into low-paying jobs without prospects, while their children were left for long hours in day-care facilities. Poverty particularly affected women and children from African-American, Hispanic, and Native American communities, whether they worked for low wages or remained on welfare. The problem persists today: women raising children alone are more likely to live in poverty than those in two-parent families.

*Below*: Living on the breadline: a Mexican immigrant mother and child in the kitchen of their mobile home in the Rio Grande Valley, Texas, in 2004.

**TURNING POINT**

### REDUCING WELFARE SUPPORT

In 1981–82, President Reagan's administration reduced payments for programs that included Aid for Dependent Children, food stamps, and Medicaid and made them more difficult to access. Reagan said welfare payments had fostered "indolence, promiscuity, casual attitudes toward marriage and divorce, and maternal indifference to child-rearing responsibilities." As a result of the cuts, the proportion of people living in poverty increased from 11.7 percent in 1979 to 15.3 percent in 1983, with huge effects on the lives of poor women and children.

# CHAPTER 5

# LAW AND POLITICS

SINCE 1980, SIGNIFICANT CHANGES IN THE LAW AND IN POLITICS have had a marked effect on women's lives. Both federal and state governments have passed laws in support of women's rights, including measures to protect against sexual harassment, domestic violence, and unequal pay. Women are better represented in politics and more women vote in elections now than ever before. However, despite all this, the U.S. government has yet to adopt the Equal Rights Amendment, first put forward by suffragists in the early 1920s.

## THE EQUAL RIGHTS AMENDMENT

By the early 1980s, the Equal Rights Amendment had become a controversial political issue. Supporters of women's rights saw it as highly important since it would, for the first time, enshrine women's

### EQUAL EARNINGS

*"The Equal Rights Amendment is much more than a symbol. It is a bread and butter issue. It means dollars and cents for women."*

NOW leaflet, 1980

*Below:* The National Organization for Women led the campaign for the ratification of the Equal Rights Amendment. In the 1980s, it focused on the practical benefits that the ERA would bring to women's lives, especially equal pay for equal work. One popular NOW badge read simply "59c"—illustrating how, on average, a woman was paid only 59 cents for every dollar paid to a man.

equality in the U.S. Constitution. Groups such as the National Organization for Women (NOW) and the ERAmerica Coalition energetically lobbied state legislatures to ratify the ERA.

There was also vocal opposition, however. Some of this came from conservatives, who believed ratification of the ERA would interfere with the rights of states to make their own laws. Some labor unions opposed it on the grounds that it would allow employers to open "men's jobs" to women, and this would drive down wages and benefits. Opponents said real equality between women and men was neither possible nor desirable. They argued that men and women had different biologies and needs.

## FEMALE OPPOSITION TO THE ERA

Perhaps surprisingly, some women were also opposed to the ERA. Leading conservative Phyllis Schlafly and her Homemakers' Union of America argued that it would deprive women of their special rights as wives and mothers. Schlafly said the ERA would remove women's welfare benefits and, most controversially, make them eligible to be drafted into the military. Some of these concerns were echoed in an opinion poll in 1978, which found that most Americans supported the ERA but that support was higher among men than women. It revealed that almost half of women were either opposed or indifferent to the ERA.

Today, anti-ERA organizers, including elements of the insurance industry and fundamentalist religious groups, argue that American women already have equal legal rights. They point to the many laws on women's rights passed by federal and state governments and to the active lobbying by women's organizations to enforce these laws.

It is hard to say whether ratification of the ERA in the 1980s would have made a real difference in the lives of American women. Many of its supporters still see its defeat

## WOMEN OF COURAGE AND CONVICTION

### WILMA MANKILLER (1945–2010)

Wilma Mankiller was the first woman to be made chief of the Cherokee Nation, based in Oklahoma. She was elected in 1985 and won several subsequent elections with overwhelming majorities. During her chiefdom, she worked to revitalize the Cherokee Nation, which suffered from poverty, unemployment, and low educational standards. Under her leadership, jobs were created in community-owned businesses, high-school education was improved, and new services such as water supplies and a hydroelectric dam were built. Mankiller also worked to restore women to their rightful, equal place in Cherokee life. She stepped down from office in 1995. In 1998, she was awarded the Presidential Medal of Freedom.

*Below:* Wilma Mankiller poses next to the tombstone of John Ross, one of the most important figures in the history of the Cherokee Nation.

*Above:* Women supporters of Barack Obama gather outside a conference center in Toledo, Ohio, three weeks before the 2008 presidential election.

TURNING POINT

## WOMEN AS VOTERS

In 1980, for the first time, young women (ages eighteen to twenty-nine) were more likely to vote than young men. In the 1972 presidential election, both groups were equally likely to vote, with a turnout of about 55 percent. In 1992, more young women were voting. Education was probably the main reason for their greater political involvement. People with a college education are more likely to vote, and today more women than men attend college.

as a significant blow to women's rights. If the ERA was adopted, discrimination on the grounds of gender would be against the law, and it would be much easier to overturn the remaining legal obstacles to female equality. Since 2007 there has been a new attempt to reintroduce the ERA in Congress—this time without a ratification deadline.

## THE FEMALE VOTE

Today women are voting in larger numbers than ever before. In the 1950s, 10 percent fewer women than men voted at elections, but after 1980 the situation reversed, with an increasing proportion of women voting. In the 2008 presidential election, 60.4 percent of women voted compared with 55.7 percent of men. For the first time, black women had the highest voter rate at 68.8 percent.

One reason for the increase in the number of women voters is that women tend to live longer than men, and older people are more likely to vote. Another reason is that women are better educated than they used to be: an increase in voter numbers is associated with higher levels of education.

Since the 1980s, an increasing number of women have moved away from voting Republican toward voting Democrat. In 1996, 11 percent more women than men voted Democrat. Researchers found that women were more likely to become politically involved if candidates were from similar backgrounds and ethnic groups as they were. For example, Barack Obama's election victory was partly the result of his appeal to black voters and to middle-class Americans, male and female.

## RUNNING FOR CONGRESS

Although women have been able to run for election to Congress since 1920, relatively few have done so. There are many reasons why. Men dominate political parties; and nomination and campaigning cost money and require political influence. Once elected, a politician will need to spend a great deal of time away from home, often working unpredictable hours. Of course, men are affected by these conditions too, but they are usually better situated to deal with them. A man often has a wife to lend support, to maintain his home, and to care for his children. He is generally freer to build up the social, political, and financial networks that will help him win nomination and election.

*Below:* When Bill Clinton became U.S. president in 1993, a total of forty-eight women were elected to Congress.

### A LONG WALK TO FREEDOM

*"She was born just a generation past slavery; a time when there were no cars on the road or planes in the sky; when someone like her couldn't vote for two reasons—because she was a woman and because of the color of her skin. . . . At a time when women's voices were silenced and their hopes dismissed, she lived to see them stand up and speak out and reach for the ballot."*

On November 5, 2008, president-elect Barack Obama paid tribute to Mrs. Nixon Ann Cooper, who at 106 years of age was one of the nation's oldest voters.

*Above*: Recent years have seen more women entering high office in U.S. politics. Here Secretary of State Condoleezza Rice votes during a United Nations Security Council meeting at the U.N. headquarters in New York in December 2008. Rice also served as national security adviser to George W. Bush from 2001–2005.

## WOMEN IN POLITICAL LIFE

Despite the obstacles to their progress, more women have been elected to political office since 1980 than ever before. In 1971, there were ten women representatives and one woman senator in the House. In 1981, the numbers had more than doubled, to twenty-one representatives and two senators.

When Bill Clinton became president in 1993, his election marked a breakthrough for women in Congress. His victory was partly a result of the support he had received from women voters. That year, forty-eight women representatives were elected to the House, together with seven senators. Since that time, there has been a general increase in the number of women in political life.

## RECORD NUMBERS

Although fewer women ran for election in 2008, more contested winnable seats. This resulted in a record number of women in Congress—seventy-three representatives and seventeen senators. There was also an increase in ethnic diversity, with twelve African-American,

*Above:* Speaker of the House Nancy Pelosi addresses journalists at a news briefing on Capitol Hill in Washington, D.C., in October 2009. Pelosi is the first woman to serve as speaker, the highest position in the House.

seven Hispanic, and two Asian-American women. All but one of them were Democrats. Prominent female senators included Barbara Boxer (Democrat), Dianne Feinstein (Democrat), and Cathy McMorris Rodgers (Republican).

In 2009, Barack Obama appointed six women to his twenty-member cabinet, including Kathleen Sebelius (secretary of health and human services), Hilda Solis (secretary of labor), and Janet Napolitano (secretary of homeland security). However, women remain very much a minority in Washington, D.C. In July 2010, they held just ninety of the 535 seats in Congress and seventeen of the one hundred seats in the Senate. In the same year, less than one-quarter of the world's political representatives at the national level were women.

At the state level, the number of women elected to office has also increased. In 1980, there were 1,426 women representatives; in 1992, there were 2,375, an increase of one-third. The numbers have since fluctuated but have not fallen below 2,200 in any year. In 2010, almost 25 percent of state legislators were women.

## " THE SKY IS THE LIMIT

"This is a historic moment—for the Congress, and for the women of this country. It is a moment for which we have waited more than 200 years. Never losing faith, we waited through the many years of struggle to achieve our rights. But women weren't just waiting; women were working. Never losing faith, we worked to redeem the promise of America, that all men and women are created equal. For our daughters and granddaughters, today, we have broken the marble ceiling. For our daughters and our granddaughters, the sky is the limit, anything is possible for them."

Nancy Pelosi, from her acceptance speech on being elected as speaker of the House of Representatives, January 2007

## FROM STATE TO STATE

The numbers of women elected vary significantly between states. In 2006, in Washington, Colorado, Maryland, Vermont, Oregon, and California, over 30 percent of legislators were women, compared with just 10 percent in South Carolina. In general, voters in states in the West and Northeast seem more prepared to elect women than those in the South and Midwest.

The most important political role at the state level is that of governor. Since 1980, more women have been elected as state governors than ever before. In the past, many women governors were the wives or widows of politicians; today they are more likely to be elected on their own merit. Recent state governors include Christine Gregoire (Washington) and Jan Brewer (Arizona). Several women governors and legislators have used their experience in state politics to build a career in Washington, D.C.

*Below:* Secretary of State Hillary Clinton meets with the president of Afghanistan, Hamid Karzai, on his visit to Washington, D.C., in May 2010.

## POLITICAL LEADERS

Women are edging closer to the U.S. presidency. The two major political parties have each nominated a woman for vice president: Geraldine Ferarro (Democrat) in 1984 and Sarah Palin (Republican) in 2008. In 2000, Senator Elizabeth Dole was a serious contender for the Republican nomination for president. In 2007–8, Senator Hillary Clinton was a leading candidate for the Democratic nomination for president. She was narrowly beaten by Barack Obama, who went on to win the presidency and who appointed her as secretary of state.

## HIGH OFFICE

In January 2007, Representative Nancy Pelosi was elected to be speaker of the House, the highest elected office in federal government and the third-highest position after president and vice president. She was the first woman to be elected to this position. Just as the number of women representatives increased after 1992, so did the number of women appointed to office. Both Republican and Democratic presidents have appointed approximately the same number of women.

Perhaps as a result of their tact and "people skills," women have been most visible in the area of foreign affairs, in the role of secretary of state. The first female secretary of state was Madeleine Albright, appointed by President Clinton in 1997. George W. Bush appointed Condoleezza Rice to the same position in 2001, and President Obama appointed Senator Hillary Clinton in 2008.

## THE LEGAL PROFESSION

Until 1980, there had never been a woman Supreme Court justice, but since then, there have been four. In 1981, Sandra Day O'Connor was appointed to the Supreme Court. Ruth Bader Ginsburg became the second woman justice in 1993. Then followed Sonia Sotomayor (the first Hispanic justice) and Elena Kagan in 2010. With the rapid entry of women into the legal profession, the number of women appointed to the Supreme Court will probably increase in future.

### BREAKTHROUGH BIOGRAPHY

**SANDRA DAY O'CONNOR (1930– )**

Sandra Day O'Connor was the first woman to become a Supreme Court justice, in 1980. After training as a lawyer in the 1950s, and despite her high academic record, only one law firm offered her a job, and that was as a legal secretary. She therefore pursued a career in public law, as an attorney and later as a judge. When she was nominated for the Supreme Court, there was considerable political opposition from some conservatives. However, in office she won praise for her exacting and unbiased judgments. She has said that, as a judge, it is her job to interpret the law rather than push for change. She decided to retire from the Supreme Court in 2005, stepping down in 2006, but continues to be active in legal and social issues.

*Below:* U.S. Supreme Court Justice Sandra Day O'Connor, pictured in 2005.

# CHAPTER 6

# WOMEN IN THE WIDER WORLD

THE VERSION OF AMERICAN WOMANHOOD MOST INSTANTLY recognized by the outside world is the one portrayed in movies and on television. Such idealized images may combine glamour, wealth, fun, and freedom. But the role of real women—for example, as diplomats, military officials, and peace campaigners—is very different from the fiction.

*Above*: Former Secretary of State Madeleine Albright about to give a speech at the Women's Conference 2009 in Long Beach, California.

## WOMEN AND DIPLOMACY

Women in government have scaled new heights in the field of foreign affairs. In 1980, Jeanne Kirkpatrick, a university professor, became national security adviser to President Reagan. From 1981 to 1985, she served as U.S. ambassador to the United Nations, the first American woman to hold this post. Two more women have since filled this

↻ **TURNING POINT**

## THE FIRST WOMAN BISHOP

In 1989, in Boston, Massachusetts, Barbara Harris became the first woman to be elected as a bishop of the Episcopal (Anglican) Church. Before her ordination as an Anglican priest in 1980, she had been active in the civil rights movement. Her views on social justice were borne out in her church work, where she was involved in projects to support minorities, poor city dwellers, and prisoners. When she retired in 2003, she was succeeded by Gayle Harris, another African-American woman.

*Right*: On February 11, 1989, Bishop Barbara Harris delivers a blessing following her ordination. Her mother stands at the left of the photograph.

role—Madeleine Albright (1993–97) and Susan Rice (2009– ). After the president and secretary of state, the U.S. ambassador to the United Nations has the most visible foreign role, especially in an international crisis, and the person in the post must be extremely tough and tenacious.

On the diplomatic level, the United States increasingly presents a female face to the world. The first woman ambassador was appointed in 1949. In the following years, there were a small number of women ambassadors, often personally appointed by the president. One such example was Clare Boothe Luce, ambassador to Italy in the 1950s. However, only a small number of women were recruited into the regular Foreign Service, and even fewer made it to ambassador. Until 1972, it was a rule that women entering the Foreign Service had to resign when they married.

Since that time, the Foreign Service has made efforts to recruit more women candidates in addition to more ethnic minorities, both in response to equal opportunities legislation and to better reflect the diversity of American life. In 1985, only 20 percent of American diplomats were women, even though the number had tripled during the 1970s. By 2005, female diplomats were 34 percent of the total, and women now outnumber men among new recruits.

♥ *WOMEN OF COURAGE AND CONVICTION*

### SWANEE HUNT

### (1950– )

Swanee Hunt served as U.S. ambassador to Austria from 1993 to 1997. During these years, Austria's southern neighbors in the former Yugoslavia were involved in a series of bitter civil wars, which resulted in the deaths of thousands of people. Hunt hosted meetings to get the enemies to talk to one another. She also organized projects to support the revival of education and culture—books for libraries, musical instruments for schools, and trees for planting in parks. In 1997, she founded the Vital Voices democracy initiative, which brought together women leaders from former conflict regions. She continues to work for peace and sexual equality at Harvard University's Kennedy School of Government.

## TURNING POINT

### THE TAILHOOK INCIDENT

In 1991, at an annual meeting of naval and marine staff known as the Tailhook Convention, eighty-three women and seven men alleged that they had been assaulted and sexually harassed. The Tailhook incident finally brought the harassment issue to public attention. The investigation that followed resulted in dismissals and blocked promotions for some high-ranking military staff and led to stricter rules against sexual harassment.

### NO ACTION

"Women serving in the U.S. military today are more likely to be raped by a fellow soldier than killed by enemy fire in Iraq. . . . At the heart of this crisis is an apparent inability or unwillingness to prosecute rapists in the ranks. . . . In nearly half of the cases investigated, the chain of command took no action: more than one third of the time, that was because of 'insufficient evidence'. . . . The Department of Defense must close this gap and remove the obstacles to effective investigation and prosecution."

In 2008, Senator Jane Harmon urges the military and government authorities to act against sex offenders.

As women diplomats have gained more experience, many have risen to high positions. In 2006, about one-third of ambassadors were women. However, the majority of the most prominent and prestigious posts are still held by men.

## WOMEN AND THE MILITARY

Since World War II, women have served in the military in women-only services, mainly as nurses and members of other support services. In 1973, the government abandoned conscription (the draft) of young men in favor of building an all-volunteer army. It disbanded women-only services and began placing women in integrated units (men and women together).

Many more military jobs and postings were opened to women, including technical and communications posts. In 1991, during the first Gulf War, 37,000 servicewomen were deployed in the Persian

*Below:* In *Private Benjamin* (1980), Goldie Hawn played a recruit in the relatively newly integrated U.S. Army. This "fish-out-of-water" movie comedy reflected attitudes to women in the military at the time.

Gulf region. After the war, the rules were changed to allow women to be engaged in frontline duties. These included supporting the troops and working on aircraft or navy vessels engaged in combat missions. Women were not allowed to take part in direct combat. In 1993, during the Clinton presidency, over one million positions were opened to women.

## OPPOSITION

The changing role of women in the military attracted considerable criticism. Some critics said that women did not have the levels of strength and resilience needed and were too emotional to cope in stressful situations. They also claimed that standards of recruitment and training had fallen and that able male candidates were turned away while their places were given to less competent females.

The argument most commonly used against women in the military was that they had a bad effect on morale. A military unit depends on discipline and teamwork, which, it is said, are more easily achieved in all-male units. Women were portrayed as a distraction, which weakened the team bonding needed during conflict. It was feared that women would seduce male soldiers, resulting in an epidemic of pregnancies.

In the early years of integration, there were allegations that young women recruits had been bullied and sexually harassed on and off duty. Reports of sexual harassment continue to this day. One survey from 2003 reported that 30 percent of women veterans said they had been raped while in the military.

## WOMEN ON THE FRONT LINE

Despite some opposition to their presence, the number of women enlisting in the military has risen rapidly. In 1970, women represented just 1.4 percent of military personnel. By 2010, this figure had risen to 15 percent.

In 2000, there were almost 200,000 women enlisted in all the armed forces, with the greatest numbers in the army and smaller numbers in the navy, air force, and marines. About half of all enlisted women are African American or from other non-white ethnic minorities.

*Below*: In 1995, female recruits undergo basic training at a U.S. Marine Corps boot camp, Parris Island, North Carolina.

*Above*: By 1996, movie images of women in the military had altered. In *Courage Under Fire*, Meg Ryan (left) played an army captain who was posthumously awarded the Medal of Honor for valor in combat during the 1991 Gulf War.

## WORK OPPORTUNITIES

Women are attracted to a military career for a range of reasons. In areas where unemployment is high, the military offers not just a steady job and salary but the opportunity to gain training and skills that may be useful once military service ends. Unlike some employers, the military does not discriminate against single mothers with young children or on racial or ethnic grounds. Recruits may be offered college scholarships and other benefits in exchange for their commitment to a military career.

Many women recruits say they are attracted by the opportunities offered for travel, adventure, and excitement. The reality is often different, with multiple postings to various bases in the United States and abroad leading to strained relationships among families. Overseas postings can be especially hard for women, who may be separated from their children for months on end.

## RECENT INVOLVEMENT

Women have participated in U.S. military interventions abroad, notably in the Balkans in the 1990s, in Afghanistan from 2001, and in Iraq from 2003. During the wars in Iraq and Afghanistan, thousands of women have served on the front line, mainly providing medical, maintenance, and logistics support. Women officers have commanded mixed or all-male units. Some women have participated in combat alongside men,

## BREAKTHROUGH BIOGRAPHY

### LIEUTENANT GENERAL CLAUDIA KENNEDY (1947– )

Claudia Kennedy joined the army in 1969 and served for thirty-one years until her retirement in 2000. She spent much of her army career in the field of military intelligence. In 1997, she was the first woman to be appointed a three-star general in the U.S. Army (women were also appointed to similar ranks in the navy, air force, and marines) and served as Army Deputy Chief of Staff for Intelligence. She has spoken out on sexual harassment of servicewomen and in 2010 was appointed Chairwoman of the Defense Advisory Committee on Women in the Services.

*Left:* Lieutenant General Claudia Kennedy, pictured in 1996.

although restrictions remain on their involvement. In 2010, it was agreed that women could serve as members of a submarine crew.

Although the posts and opportunities have increased, most women have remained in more traditional roles. In 2000, over 70 percent of medical and support personnel were women. In other areas, there were fewer women—they constituted only 18 percent of those undertaking technical roles (such as engineering and communications) and just 6.6 percent of those in combat or other frontline roles.

## VOLUNTEERING

Women's involvement in the wider world also includes volunteer work, in projects at home and abroad. Working voluntarily for nonprofit organizations and charities gives a sense of purpose and fulfilment and may provide an opportunity to learn about international issues. It can include work in schools. Alternatively,

### REAL BONDING

"People talk about male bonding in the military and how female soldiers supposedly will disrupt unit cohesion. Real bonding, however, goes far beyond whether the people involved are two men or two women or one of each. . . . Going to war with a unit, risking your life with them, builds an intimate and intense relationship. The soldiers don't all have to be men for that to happen."

Major Rhonda Cornum, the only female officer to become a prisoner of war during the First Gulf War.

volunteers may have particular skills to offer that will improve the quality of people's lives. At international work camps, volunteers can meet, live, work, learn, and exchange ideas and skills with local people. The issues addressed by volunteers may include education, environmental conservation, cultural heritage, social justice, and rural and human development.

## WOMEN IN THE PEACE MOVEMENT

Just as women have entered the military in record numbers, so there are groups of women who have organized against the military. In the early 1980s, when the Cold War was at its height, the main concern of these women was the threat of nuclear war, especially the deployment of cruise missiles equipped with nuclear warheads. In November 1980, hundreds of women circled the Pentagon, the headquarters of the

Department of Defense, to protest against the deployment of nuclear weapons.

In 1983, inspired by the example of women's peace camps in Europe, women established similar camps in the United States. Women in Washington state formed the Puget Sound Peace Camp, near the Boeing Aerospace Center, where cruise missiles were being manufactured. In New York state, women set up camp in Seneca, where the cruise missiles were believed to be stored. Both peace camps were women only, in the belief that this made them safer and more peaceful. Both remained for several years, with women activists courting arrest through non-violent activities, including entering the production plant and military base and distributing leaflets to workers and military personnel.

## ACTIVITIES ABROAD

Following the end of the Cold War in the 1990s, the women's peace movement focused on other aspects of U.S. foreign policy. In the 1980s, women peace activists traveled to Central America to oppose the support being given by the United States to right-wing governments there. Women were active in campaigns against the First Gulf War of 1991. However, the most concerted opposition came at the start of the 21st century in response to American-led interventions in Afghanistan and Iraq. In both conflicts, the number of soldiers killed and injured aroused public opposition.

In 2005, Cindy Sheehan, mother of one of the soldiers to die in Iraq, organized a mothers' group to oppose the war and rapidly became a figurehead for the peace movement. Like the earlier peace campaigners, she set up her own camp, close to President Bush's Texas ranch. While she gained much support, she also became a hate figure for pro-war groups. She traveled widely, courting arrest and speaking against the war. In 2008, she ran for Congress as an independent anti-war candidate, but lost to Nancy Pelosi.

*Left*: In September 2005, anti-war activist Cindy Sheehan (center) speaks on Capitol Hill in Washington, D.C., urging Congress and President George W. Bush to remove U.S. troops from Iraq.

## TURNING POINT

### DEATHS IN EL SALVADOR

In December 1980, four American women, three nuns and a missionary, were brutally beaten and murdered by a military death squad in El Salvador. The women had been working in the city slums, assisting refugees who had fled their homes to escape the civil war then raging. The murders shocked many Americans, bringing the conflicts in Central America to national attention. Public outrage forced the U.S. government to put pressure on the El Salvador government to identify and punish the murderers. Twenty years later, in 2000, two former generals were cleared of the murders and no action has since been taken.

*Below*: In December 1980, three American nuns pray over the bodies of the four women who were kidnapped and executed by the military in El Salvador.

# CHAPTER 7

# ARTS AND CULTURE

WOMEN HAVE LONG BEEN PROMINENT IN THE ARTS WORLD. They have written books and articles in magazines, newspapers, and online. They have made their mark in music, film, and on television. Celebrities such as Oprah Winfrey and Barbara Walters have had a significant impact on the attitudes of the American people as a whole and wielded a power unimagined by women from earlier periods of history.

## NEWS AND CURRENT AFFAIRS

A number of women journalists have risen to prominence in the past two decades. They include Katie Couric, anchor and managing editor of *CBS Evening News*. Couric co-hosted NBC's *Today* from 1991 until 2006 and has been nicknamed "America's Sweetheart" as a result of her ratings popularity. *The CBS Evening News with Katie Couric* won

### WOMEN OF COURAGE AND CONVICTION

#### BARBARA WALTERS
#### (1929– )

Barbara Walters is a prominent female news anchor and interviewer. She began her television career as a "Today Girl" in the early 1960s and went on to become one of America's leading political interviewers. She is best known for her interviews on ABC's *20/20* and has covered presidential elections and the aftermath of 9/11. Her career has spanned over fifty years, and she is one of the few women allowed to "age on air." Walters semi-retired as a broadcast journalist in 2004 but continues as an occasional correspondent.

*Right:* Journalist Barbara Walters, pictured in 2009.

the 2008 and 2009 Edward R. Murrow Award for best newscast, and on March 29, 2009, Couric was awarded with the Emmy Governor's Award for her broadcasting career. Christiane Amanpour, anchor of *This Week* for ABC News, is one of the most recognized international correspondents on American television. Highlights of her work in dangerous conflict zones include coverage of the First Gulf War (1991), and the Bosnian War (1992–95).

## THE OPRAH EFFECT

In 1984, a new host took over a low-rated television talk show. Her name was Oprah Winfrey, and she was an immediate success. Oprah's gender, racial identity, and working-class background were a unique combination. She was an African-American woman who had overcome a childhood of poverty and abuse to make her way in the tough media world. She became a role model for ordinary, aspiring women everywhere, proving that with courage and determination they could achieve wealth and success.

## TV DRAMA ROLES

Roles for women in television drama reflect changing attitudes over the years. The 1980s were the heyday of big-budget family sagas such as *Dallas* and *Dynasty*. Both series featured strong women taking on men in business and in the bedroom. Since then, family drama has tended to have a more serious or realistic take on life, and although women still play leading roles, they rarely capture the public imagination in the same way.

Comedy drama has also provided women with a wide range of roles to showcase their talents. The hit show *Roseanne*, the creation of comedian Roseanne Barr, ran from 1988 to 1997. It portrayed the life of the Connors, a blue-collar family in small-town America, with working parents and temperamental teenagers. It featured a range

> ## TELLING THE STORY
>
> *"There are some situations one simply cannot be neutral about, because when you are neutral you are an accomplice. Objectivity doesn't mean treating all sides equally. It means giving each side a hearing."*
>
> News journalist Christiane Amanpour's response to accusations of political bias toward Bosnian Muslims during her coverage of the Siege of Sarajevo.

*Below*: Over the years, the comedy TV show *Roseanne* tackled taboo subjects such as drug abuse, teenage pregnancy, obesity, and domestic violence.

TURNING POINT

## CAGNEY AND LACEY

*Cagney and Lacey* was one of the premier drama series of the 1980s. Running from 1982 to 1988, it told the story of two New York female detectives and their fight against crime and sexism in the masculine world of the precinct. Christine Cagney (Sharon Gless) was an ambitious career woman, happily single and dating a succession of eligible men. Mary Beth Lacey (Tyne Daly) was married with two (later three) children and was the main family breadwinner. *Cagney and Lacey* was much more than another cop show—it was the first drama series to star two women and highlighted issues such as domestic violence, child abuse, and the impact of breast cancer.

of strong female characters, with Roseanne the most outrageous and outspoken of all. For many Americans, the show offered a recognizable slice of life.

The hit comedy series of the 1990s was *Friends*, which ran from 1994 to 2004. Set in a stylish apartment and a fashionable coffee shop in Manhattan, it revolved around the lives of six young people in their twenties—three women and three men. Rachel was a fashion editor, Monica a chef, and Phoebe a masseuse and musician. As its title suggests, the show dealt with themes such as love and friendship, particularly male-female relations in the modern world. The script was witty, and many young women saw elements in the friends' fictional lives that echoed their own.

## CITY WOMEN

At the turn of the 21st century, *Sex and the City*, also set in Manhattan, featured four women, three in their thirties and one in her forties. Although they had high-flying careers, their main interest

*Below*: In *Sex and the City*, the four female characters discussed romance and sex in an up-front way. The show examined how changing roles and expectations affected women's lives at the turn of the millennium.

in life was fashion and men. Carrie, the most fashionable of them all, used her life and the lives of her friends as the basis for her newspaper column. The series broke new ground in the way it depicted women's search for happiness and sexual adventures. It was aimed at women, and men were marginal figures, often of fun or derision. In most respects, *Sex and the City*, which ran from 1998 to 2004, was the polar opposite of *Roseanne*, but like *Roseanne*, it showed female friendship as a central feature of modern life.

## WOMEN IN THE MOVIE INDUSTRY

Opportunities for women to take control in the movie industry are still few. One industry survey found that in 2007, women made up only 6 percent of directors, 22 percent of producers, 10 percent of writers, 17 percent of editors, and 2 percent of cinematographers. However, women have had success, particularly in the independent film sector, producing and directing low-budget feature films and documentaries.

A few women have become successful mainstream Hollywood directors. They include Susan Seidelman (*Desperately Seeking Susan*), Penny Marshall (*A League of Their Own*), Sofia Coppola (*Lost in Translation*), and Kathryn Bigelow (*The Hurt Locker*). Actors Jodie Foster and Diane Keaton have also made the transition to become successful directors.

**TURNING POINT**

## RECOGNITION AT THE OSCARS

In 2010, Kathryn Bigelow became the first woman to win the Best Director award at the American Academy of Motion Picture Arts and Sciences annual awards (Oscars). She won the Oscar for her film *The Hurt Locker*, which was also voted Best Picture. Bigelow started her directing career in the 1980s. Unusually for a female director, she mostly makes action pictures, focusing on male characters in difficult and violent situations.

*Below*: Director Kathryn Bigelow proves that women can succeed in the highly competitive, male-dominated world of Hollywood movie-making.

## BREAKTHROUGH BIOGRAPHY

### CINDY SHERMAN (1954– )

Cindy Sherman is an acclaimed photographer, filmmaker, and, most unusually, a model in her own photographs. She began her photography series called *Complete Untitled Film Stills* in 1977 depicting herself in different guises and locations. Her work since then has taken many forms, but her main subject remains women and the way society sees them, and she continues to photograph herself in surprising and sometimes bizarre ways. She has said: "I feel I'm anonymous in my work. When I look at the pictures, I never see myself; they aren't self-portraits. Sometimes I disappear."

### WOMEN IN CRIME FICTION

"*What began as a trickle of strong women a century ago . . . has grown into a great outpouring of women's stories. Marcia Muller gave us Sharon McCone in 1977. Five years later Sue Grafton and I flung Kinsey Millhone and V. I. Warshawski onto an unsuspecting world: English PI [private eye] Anna Lee joined us at the same time. Since then the number of women heroes has grown past counting.*"

Sara Paretsky, creator of Chicago private eye V. I. Warshawski, 1992. In crime fiction, women authors have developed a new type of female protagonist—tough, intelligent, and feisty.

## MOVIE STARS

Along with pop stars, stars of film and television have been the most potent cultural icons in the United States, and some of the best-known stars are female. However, there are significant differences in the experiences of male and female movie stars. Few women are deemed "bankable" enough to "open" a movie—in other words, it is not believed that a female star can attract moviegoers on the strength of her name alone—and few get top billing. Women on screen are expected to be young and beautiful, and this restricts the roles available to them and limits their movie career.

## SURVIVORS

A few female actors have contradicted the trend. The outstanding example is Meryl Streep, who began her movie career in the 1970s and is still playing leading roles thirty-five years later. Glenn Close and Sigourney Weaver have also successfully chosen roles that highlight their intelligence and talents, while Shirley MacLaine and Kathy Bates have had long careers playing largely "character" roles.

*Below*: Meryl Streep, pictured in 2010 with the Golden Globe award she received for her performance in *Julie and Julia*.

## WOMEN WRITERS

Among the most celebrated authors of the past thirty years are Joyce Carol Oates, Annie Proulx, and Jane Smiley. In addition, women are prominent in literary criticism, with Susan Sontag, for example, writing on subjects as varied as photography, illness, and politics. Although ethnic minority women had been writing for years, they had generally been ignored, unrecognized, or limited to their own communities. However, during the last decades of the 20th century, their writings were increasingly encouraged, published, and marketed to a wider American audience.

The most prominent African-American writer is Toni Morrison, whose early works focused on the experiences of individual black women in a white-dominated society. In the 1980s, her writing expanded in scope to explore the legacies of slavery, racism, and sexism in both white and black communities.

Alice Walker's *The Color Purple*, was the first novel by a black woman to win a Pulitzer Prize. It tells of a young woman growing up amid poverty and abuse in 1930s Georgia. Other women writers include bell hooks (the pen name of Gloria Jean Watkins), a poet and philosopher; poet Louise Glück, who won the 1993 Pulitzer Prize for Poetry for *The Wild*

*Above:* Writer and winner of the 1994 Pulitzer Prize Annie Proulx poses for photographers during the launch of her novel *Brokeback Mountain*.

### TURNING POINT

### *BELOVED*

Toni Morrison's novel *Beloved*, published in 1987 and later made into a movie, won a Pulitzer Prize in 1988 and in 2006 was named best American novel of the past twenty-five years by the *New York Times Book Review*. It was one of the achievements for which she was awarded the Nobel Prize for Literature in 1993. She was only the second American woman to have been given this award.

## TINA TURNER (1939– )

In the 1960s and 1970s, singer Tina Turner was a pop star in a duo with her husband, Ike. However, the relationship was abusive, and after an acrimonious divorce, Turner set out to reinvent herself as a solo artist, recording and touring. In 1984, her single "What's Love Got to Do With It" reached number one on the charts, and other hits followed. Turner was an unusual star—black and female and middle aged. Her gutsy, flamboyant style and spectacular stage shows won her a legion of new fans. She remained a star, recording, touring, and taking movie roles, into the 21st century.

*Right:* Singer Tina Turner, performing in Paris, France, in 1990.

*Iris*; and Rita Dove, the first African American to be appointed as Poet Laureate Consultant in Poetry to the Library of Congress.

Women from other ethnic backgrounds have also brought their experiences to wider audiences. Maxine Hong Kingston and Amy Tan write of Chinese-American experiences, Hisaye Yamamoto of Japanese Americans, and Helena María Viramontes of Hispanics. Leslie Marmon Silko writes of the Laguna Pueblo people of the Southwest and Louise Erdrich of the struggle of the Native American communities on a North Dakota reservation.

## MUSICIANS

Music is probably the most widely known aspect of modern American culture, and it reaches a global audience. In classical music, while opera singers such as Jessye Norman and Renée Fleming have gained worldwide fame, there are few women conductors, directors, or composers. In 2010, less than 10 percent of conductors were women. The best known include JoAnn Falletta of the Buffalo Philharmonic

Orchestra and Marin Alsop of the Baltimore Symphony Orchestra. In 1983, Ellen Taaffe Zwilich became the first female composer to receive a Pulitzer Prize for music.

## COUNTRY AND JAZZ

In terms of popular music, country-and-western music and jazz spring directly from American traditions, and women have a prominent role in both. In country music, women have achieved recognition as singers, musicians, and songwriters, and some, such as Dolly Parton, Crystal Gayle, Billie Jo Spears, and Sheryl Crowe, have crossed into mainstream music. In the male-dominated world of jazz music, a number of gifted vocalists, including Helen Merrill, Dianne Reeves, Jane Monheit, and pianist and vocalist Diana Krall, have made their mark.

## POP MUSIC

The 1980s brought music videos and the cable television channel MTV, which showcased new female pop artists. Two of the biggest names were Tina Turner and Madonna, both of whom achieved fame in the early 1980s and remained stars in the following decades.

**IN CHARGE**

"I may be dressing like the typical bimbo but I'm in charge. . . . People don't think of me as a person who is not in charge of my career or my life. And isn't that what feminism is all about? Aren't I in charge of my life, doing the things I want to do, making my own decisions?"

Madonna, speaking on ABC-Lifetime, December 1991

*Left:* Madonna performing early in her career in Seattle in 1985. Her enduring success is largely the result of a combination of talent, opportunism, and determination.

# CHAPTER 8

# THE PERIOD IN BRIEF

UNLIKE THE 1960S AND 1970S, THE YEARS OF THE CIVIL RIGHTS movement and women's liberation, the 1980s to 2000s did not represent an upheaval in terms of women's history. However, major advances were made by individual women following those earlier years of change. At work, women have increasingly moved into traditionally "male" jobs and now hold positions of greater authority than they did three decades ago. In daily life, they are better educated and have greater equality.

## " 

### THE WOMEN'S CENTURY

*"Women will run the 21st century. . . . This is going to be the women's century and young people are going to be its leaders."*

Bella Abzug (1920–98), speaking in April 1998, predicts a feminist future after a lifetime of battling for equal rights for women.

*Above:* Making a mark in the business world: Marilyn Carlson (right), chairman and chief executive officer of Carlson Companies, Inc., one of the largest privately held companies in the world, receives a business award from Jordan's Queen Noor during the Women's World Awards gala in Vienna, March 5, 2009.

## MOVING FORWARD

In Congress, women now make up 20 percent of the total number of representatives and senators, compared with less than 5 percent in 1980. This marked improvement is still a long way from gender equality since women make up 51 percent of the U.S. population. A few women have been elected to high political office, and women legislators have helped bring new laws into effect to try to ensure women are treated equally—

although in practice this does not always happen. However, there is still no Equal Rights Amendment to the Constitution, and violence against women in the home and on the streets remains a concern.

## WORK AND HOME LIFE

Perhaps the enduring but little noticed changes in this period have been the gradual shifts taking place in women's everyday lives. Since 1980, women have become better educated, more work and career oriented, and more equal and assertive in the workplace. They have married later, or not married at all, and on average have given birth to fewer children. In the home, they have gained more equality with their partners, although they usually still have primary responsibility for housework and child care. Many have joined the military and fought on the front line beside men. The poorest women have not benefited so greatly from such changes, but for the majority, there have been new prospects and opportunities.

In the 1960s and 1970s, mainstream society found the ideas put forward by the women's liberation movement deeply controversial and unsettling. Today most of those ideas, such as equal pay, equal work opportunities, and equality within the home, are generally accepted, even if they have not always been put into practice. However, some people might argue that society has become more sexist, citing the easy access to pornography and the sexualization of young girls as backward steps.

Success has in itself changed female aspirations. Women are striving to overcome obstacles and find their own way through life, overcoming not just physical and financial barriers but also the stereotypical ideas of what they are and what they can achieve. In spite of some setbacks along the way, the process of women achieving their full potential continues apace.

### WOMEN OF COURAGE AND CONVICTION

#### SUSAN SOLOMON (1956– )

Susan Solomon is an internationally renowned scientist working in one of the pioneering areas of science—understanding climate change. Working with the National Oceanic and Atmospheric Administration (NOAA), Solomon developed breakthrough research into how chemicals affect Earth's atmosphere. Her research led to a global ban on chemicals that destroy the ozone layer. Among other honors, an Antarctic glacier has been named after her.

*Below*: First Lady Michelle Obama reads aloud to a group of young children during a visit to the Department of Labor's Child Development Center in Washington, D.C., in January 2010.

# TIMELINE

**1977**     The National Conference for Women takes place in Houston, Texas, and lays the framework for legal and other changes for women.

**1980**     The United Nations Conference on Women in Copenhagen, Denmark, is held to assess progress halfway through the United Nations Decade for Women (1975–85).
President Ronald Reagan takes office.
For the first time, more women than men enroll at college.

**1981**     Sandra Day O'Connor becomes the first woman to be appointed to the U.S. Supreme Court.
Jeanne Kirkpatrick is appointed U.S. ambassador to the United Nations—the first woman to hold this post.

**1982**     The Equal Rights Amendment (ERA) lapses after not enough states ratify it. The ERA had proposed a new amendment to the U.S. Constitution outlawing discrimination on the grounds of sex. It had been accepted by Congress in 1972 and passed to the states for ratification. Despite the extra time granted, only thirty-five of the thirty-eight states agreed to ratify the ERA.
Publication of *The Color Purple*, by Alice Walker, who later becomes the first African-American woman to win the Pulitzer Prize.

**1983**     Sally Ride becomes the first American woman astronaut on a *Challenger* mission.

**1984**     Oprah Winfrey begins her career as a talk-show host in Chicago.
Geraldine Ferraro is nominated as the vice-presidential candidate by the Democratic Party. She is the first woman to be selected for this position by either of the two main parties.

**1985**     Ronald Reagan begins his second term as president.
Wilma Mankiller is elected chief of the Cherokee Nation of Oklahoma, the first woman to lead a major Native American tribe.
The third U.N. Conference for Women is held in Nairobi, Kenya.

**1988**     *Roseanne* begins its hit run on television.

**1989**     President George H.W. Bush takes office.
Reverend Barbara Harris becomes the first woman elected as bishop of the Episcopal Church.
The Berlin Wall falls and communism collapses in Eastern Europe.

**1991**     In the First Gulf War, American troops lead multinational forces against Iraq; 37,000 American women serve in the war.
The Tailhook incident brings the sexual harassment of women in the military to national attention.
The movie *Thelma and Louise*, a story of female friendship, is released.

**1993**     Bill Clinton takes office, becoming the first Democratic president in twelve years. In the Congressional elections, the largest-ever numbers of women are elected to both houses.

The first Take Our Daughters to Work Day is held to help overcome gender stereotypes about jobs. It later becomes an annual event.

1993    Ruth Bader Ginsburg becomes the second woman to be appointed a Supreme Court justice. President Clinton opens over one million positions in the military to women, leaving only a small number of roles (mainly in frontline combat) closed to them. Toni Morrison is awarded the Nobel Prize for Literature.

1994    *Friends* starts its run on U.S. television; it continues until 2004.

1995    The fourth U.N. Conference for Women is held in Beijing, China, together with a parallel conference of women activists from nongovernmental organizations. Thousands of women from all over the world participate, including many Americans.

1997    President Clinton starts his second term of office and appoints Madeleine Albright as secretary of state. The first women are appointed as three-star generals in the army, navy, air force, and marines.

1998    *Sex and the City* begins its run on U.S. television; it continues until 2004.

2001    President George W. Bush of the Republican Party takes office after a tight election and a controversial Supreme Court judgment in his favor. On September 11, almost 3,000 people die when hijacked planes crash into landmarks in New York and Washington, D.C. An Islamic group called Al Qaeda claims responsibility.

2003    U.S.-led forces launch a military attack on Iraq.

2005    President Bush starts his second term of office with Condoleezza Rice as secretary of state, the first African-American woman to hold such a high-profile position.

2007    Nancy Pelosi becomes the first woman speaker of the House of Representatives and the highest-ranking female politician in U.S. history.

2008    Hillary Clinton, a former first lady, campaigns for the Democratic Party nomination for president, eventually losing to Barack Obama. Sarah Palin is nominated as candidate for vice president by the Republican Party. In national elections, a record number of women are elected to Congress: seventy-four representatives and seventeen senators.

2009    Barack Obama takes office as the first African-American president. Hillary Clinton becomes secretary of state. Sonia Sotomayor becomes the third woman to be appointed as a justice of the Supreme Court and the first of Hispanic origin.

2010    Kathryn Bigelow becomes the first woman to win an Academy Award for Best Director for *The Hurt Locker,* which wins also an Academy Award for Best Picture. The secretary of defense announces that servicewomen can work on a submarine crew, a position previously barred to them.

# GLOSSARY AND FURTHER INFORMATION

**anorexia** An emotional disorder, expressed in terms of a refusal to eat and an obsession with weight loss.

**astrolabe** An early instrument used to make astronomical measurements.

**Botox** A chemical so-called "anti-aging" preparation used for the treatment of wrinkles, mainly in the face.

**bulimia** An emotional disorder characterized by compulsive overeating, usually followed by self-induced vomiting.

**civil rights** Equal social and political rights.

**civil war** A war between opposing groups of people of the same country.

**Cold War** The period from the end of World War II in 1945 to the fall of the Berlin Wall in 1989. During this time, the world was divided politically into capitalist countries, led by the United States, and communist countries, led by the Union of Socialist Soviet Republics, or USSR (present-day Russia was a part of the USSR).

**communism** A system where the state (government) owns and controls most industry and other activities and the government is usually a one-party state, without opposition parties.

**conscription** A system in which all young men (sometimes young women also) are required to register for service in the military.

**conservative** A person, political party, or view of the world that prefers traditional values and that opposes much social or political change.

**contraception** Medical or other ways of preventing unwanted pregnancy; also referred to as birth control or family planning.

**corporate** Owned by a company or referring to company values.

**cruise missile** A military missile, sometimes equipped with a nuclear warhead, that can travel for thousands of miles to reach an enemy target.

**deployment** Putting something into action; in the context used in this book, sending military personnel into conflict.

**diabetes** A disorder characterized by excessive thirst and the production of large amounts of urine.

**feminism** The values and ideas that support female equality with males.

**foreclosure** When a home or business is taken from the owners, usually because of debts owed.

**gender equality** The goal of achieving equal opportunities between men and women.

**HIV/AIDS** AIDS (Acquired Immune Deficiency Syndrome) is an infectious disease caused by the Human Immunodeficiency Virus (HIV).

**immigrant** A person who moves to another country to live.

**labor union** An organization that has as its main aim the protection of the pay and working conditions of its members.

**lesbian** A woman who is sexually attracted to other women.

**logistics** A system of organizing activities in a planned and logical way.

**mortgage** A long-term loan, usually by a bank, to a person to buy a house or an apartment.

**neurosurgeon** A physician trained in surgery of the nervous system and who specializes in brain surgery.

**ordination** The official appointment of a priest, minister or rabbi.

**political asylum** Protection from arrest given by the government of one country to political refugees from another country.

**posthumously** After death.

**pro choice** Believing that a woman should be able to decide freely whether to end a pregnancy.

**prosecuting** Conducting a war.

**ratify** To agree and sign a law or international treaty by government, which gives it final approval.

**right wing** In political terms, an individual or outlook in support of capitalism or free enterprise; in general terms, a more conservative outlook on the world.

**service industries** Industries that offer services (such as health, education, or retail) rather than goods (such as agriculture or manufacturing).

**stereotype** A common belief about a type of person that is often untrue.

**taboo** Something that is banned on grounds of morality or taste.

**welfare** Financial support provided by the government for people who need it.

**women's liberation** A revival and rethinking of feminist thought and activity that began in the mid-1960s and continued to the end of the 1970s.

BOOKS

Collins, Gail. *When Everything Changed: The Amazing Journey of American Women from 1960 to the Present.* New York: Little, Brown, 2009.

Finlay, Barbara. *George W. Bush and the War on Women.* London: Zed Books, 2006.

Greer, Germaine. *The Whole Woman.* London: Transworld Publishers, 1999.

Kipnis, Laura. *The Female Thing: Dirt, Sex, Envy, Vulnerability.* London: Serpent's Tail, 2007.

Millett, Kate. *Sexual Politics.* London: Virago Press, 2003 (reprinted).

Rosenberg, Rosalind. *Divided Lives: American Women in the Twentieth Century.* London: Penguin, 1993.

Rowbotham, Sheila. *A Century of Women: The History of Women in Britain and the United States.* London: Penguin, 1999.

Walter, Natasha. *The New Feminism.* London: Virago Press, 1999.

Ware, Susan, ed. *Notable American Women: A Biographical Dictionary Completing the Twentieth Century.* Cambridge, Massachusetts: Belknap Press, 2004.

WEB SITES

www.cawp.rutgers.edu/
www1.cuny.edu/portal_ur/content/womens_leadership/index.html
http://feminism.eserver.org/
www.guttmacher.org/
www.jofreeman.com/photos/IWY1977.html
http://pewresearch.org/

# INDEX

FEB    2012